Every Sunday
(MGM short, 1936)

PLATE 1

The Wizard of Oz
(MGM, 1939)
Costume designer: Adrian

Strike Up the Band
(MGM, 1940)
Costume designer: Dolly Tree

PLATE 2

For Me and My Gal
(MGM, 1942)
Costume designer: Robert Kalloch

Life Begins for Andy Hardy
(MGM, 1941)
Costume designer: Robert Kalloch

PLATE 3

Two costumes from
Ziegfeld Girl
(MGM, 1941)
Costume designer: Adrian

PLATE 4

Two more costumes from
Ziegfeld Girl

PLATE 5

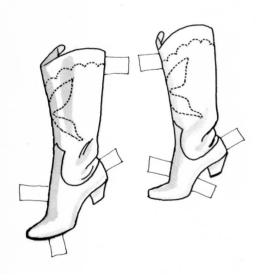

Girl Crazy
(MGM, 1943)
Costume designer: Irene, in association with Irene Sharaff

Babes on Broadway
(MGM, 1941)
Costume designer: Robert Kalloch

PLATE 6

Meet Me in St. Louis
(MGM, 1944)
Costume designer: Irene Sharaff, supervised by
Irene

PLATE 7

Two more costumes from
Meet Me in St. Louis

PLATE 8

Two costumes from
The Harvey Girls
(MGM, 1946)
Costume designer: Helen Rose, supervised by Irene

PLATE 9

Ziegfeld Follies
(MGM, 1946)
Costume designer: Helen Rose, supervised by Irene

As the blonde Marilyn Miller in
Till the Clouds Roll By
(MGM, 1946)
Costume designer: Helen Rose, supervised by Irene

PLATE 10

The Pirate
(MGM, 1948)
Costume designer: Tom Keogh, supervised by Irene

Easter Parade
(MGM, 1948)
Costume designer: Irene

PLATE 11

Words and Music
(MGM, 1948)
Costume designer: Helen Rose

From *Easter Parade*

PLATE 12

In the Good Old Summertime
(MGM, 1949)
Costume designer: Irene

Summer Stock
(MGM, 1950)
Costume designer: Walter Plunkett

PLATE 13

Two costumes from
A Star Is Born
(Warners, 1954)
Costume designers: Jean Louis, Mary Ann Nyberg,
Irene Sharaff

PLATE 14

"Get Happy" costume from
Summer Stock
reworn by Judy in concert at
Las Vegas, 1957

A Child Is Waiting
(Stanley Kramer, 1963)
Costume designer: Howard Shoup

Judgment at Nuremberg
(Stanley Kramer, 1961)
Costume designer: Jean Louis

PLATE 15

I Could Go On Singing
(Barbican–United Artists, 1963)
Costume designer: Edith Head

At Home at the Palace
(live appearance in N.Y., 1967)

PLATE 16